# Blank Comic Book

## for Drawing & Sketching

# This Comic Book
### created by :

........................................................................

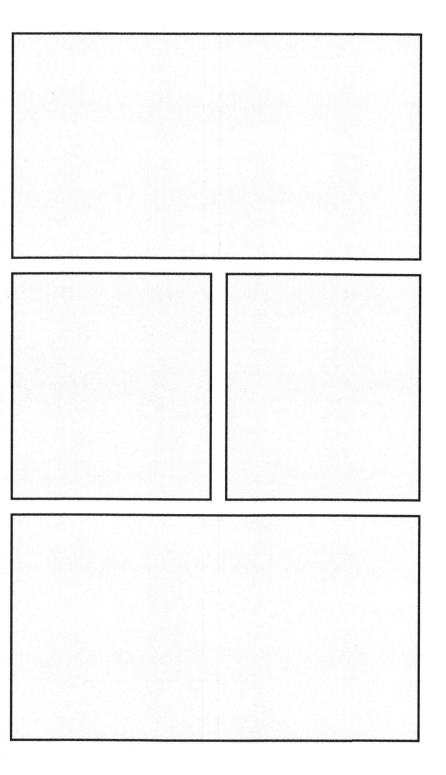

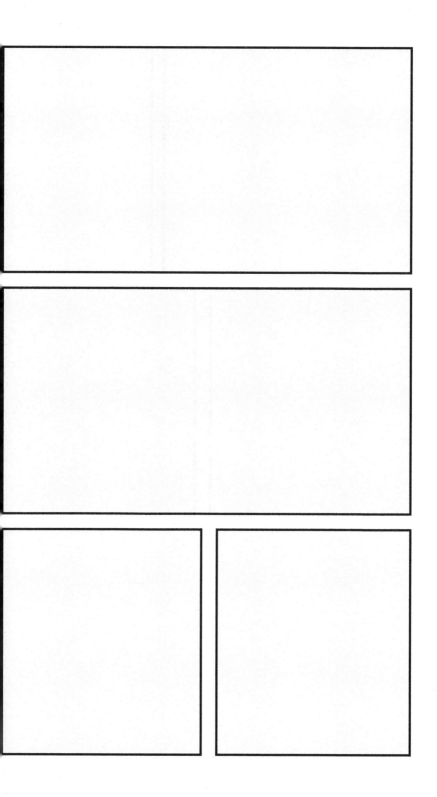

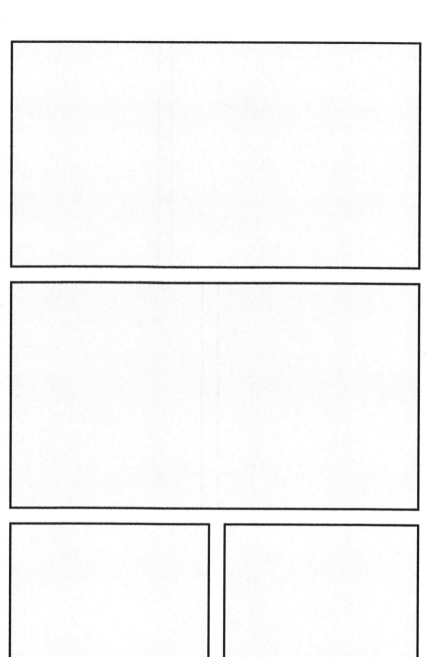

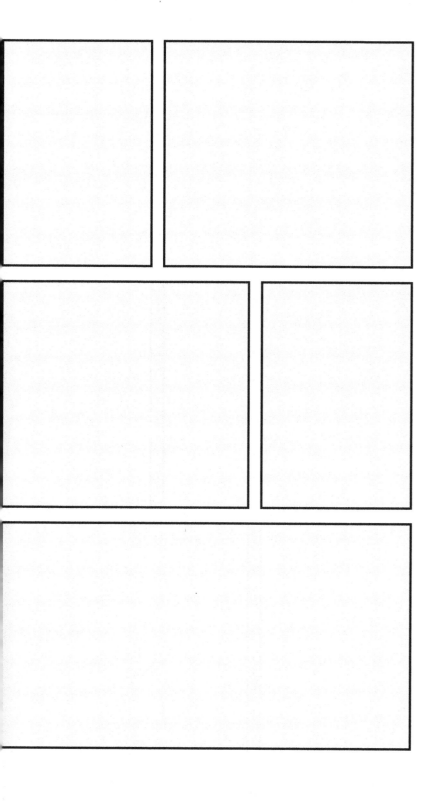

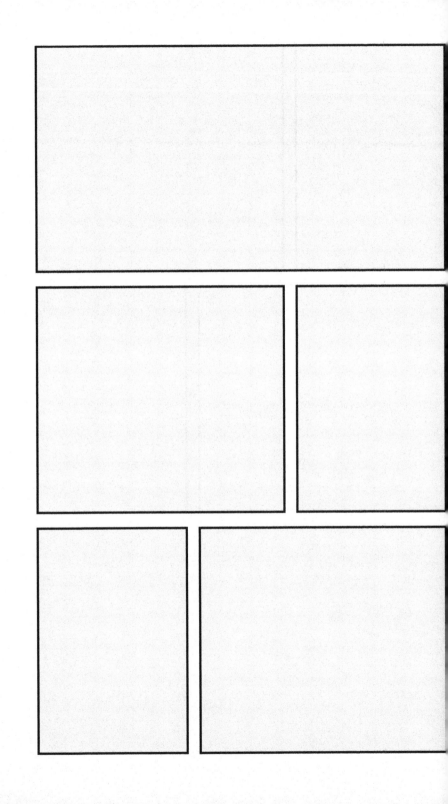

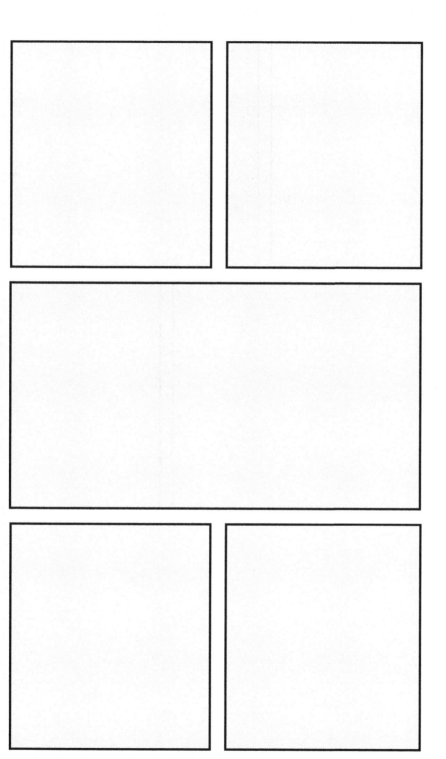

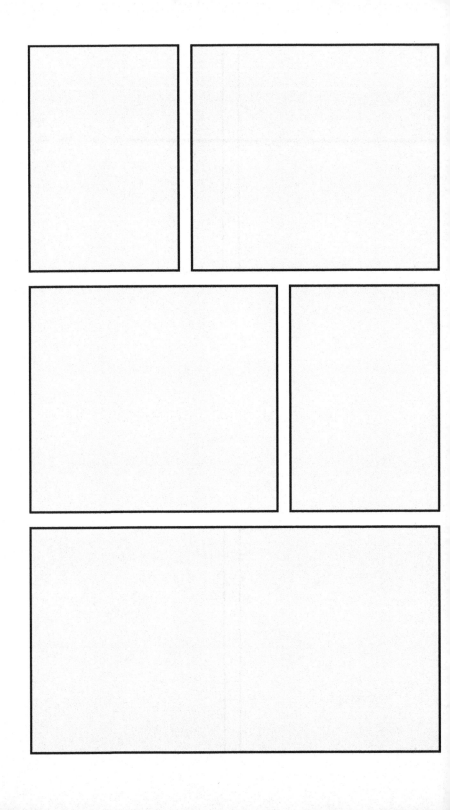

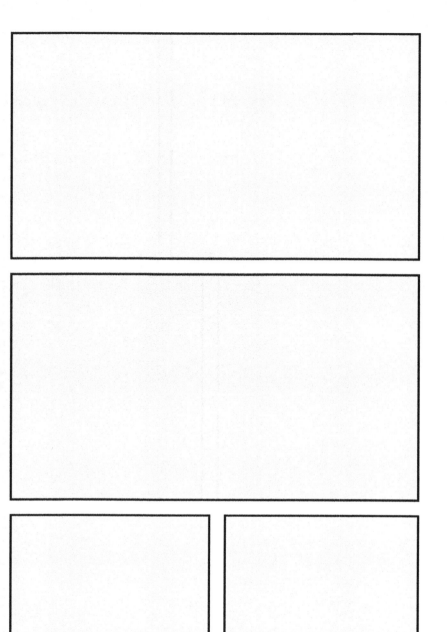

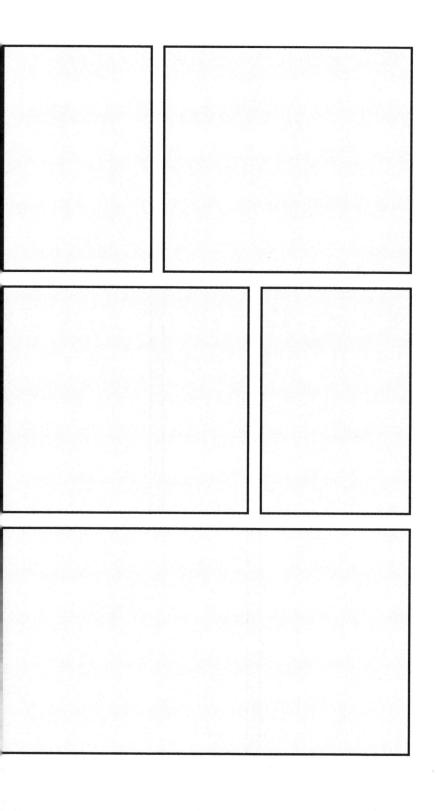

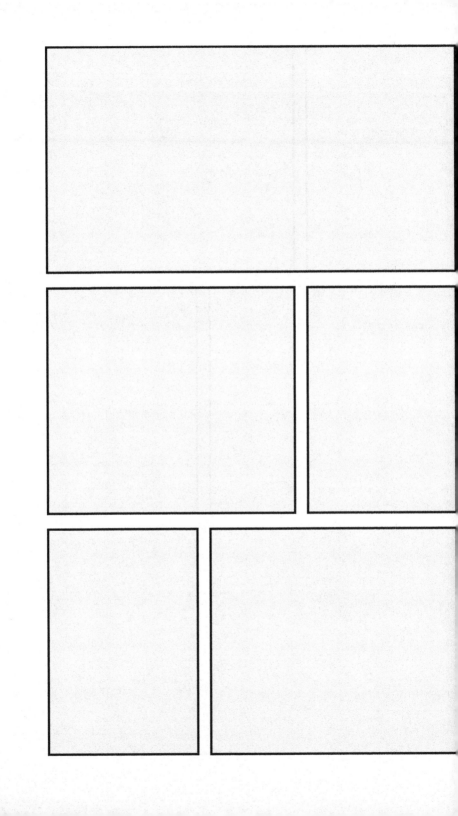

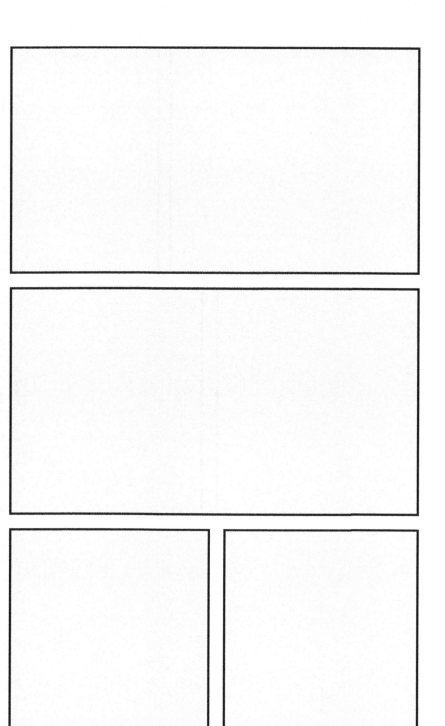

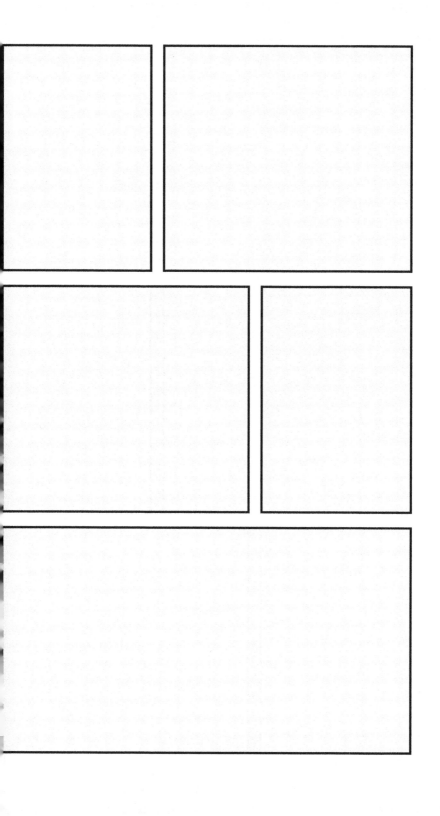

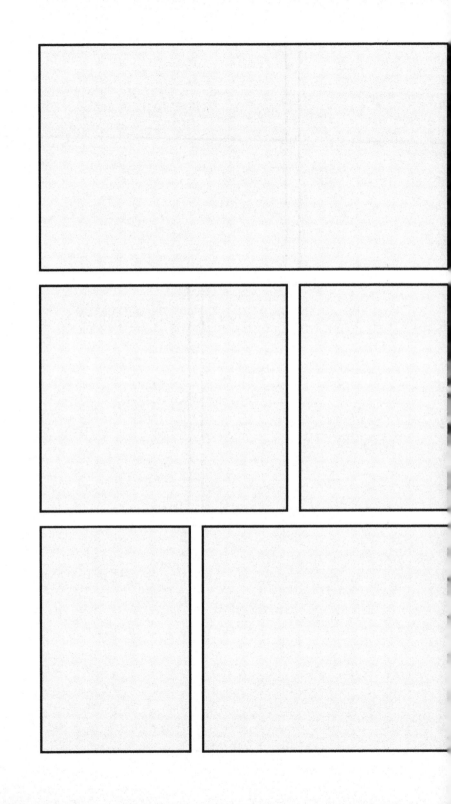

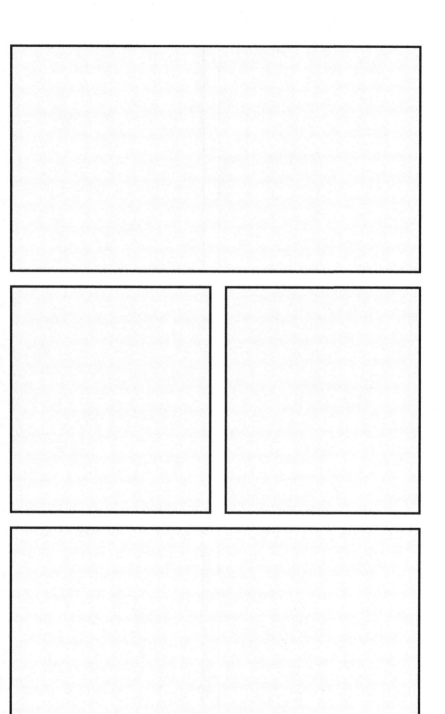

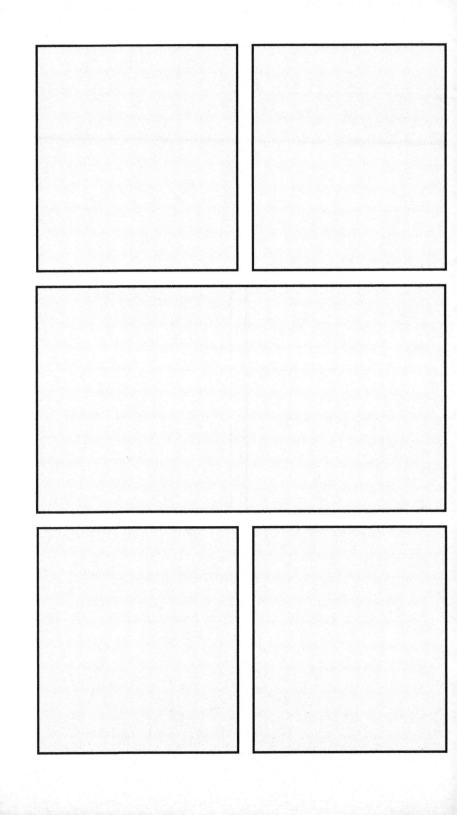

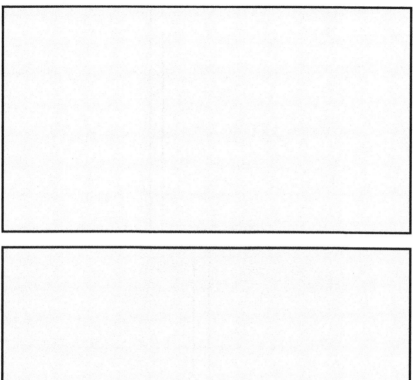

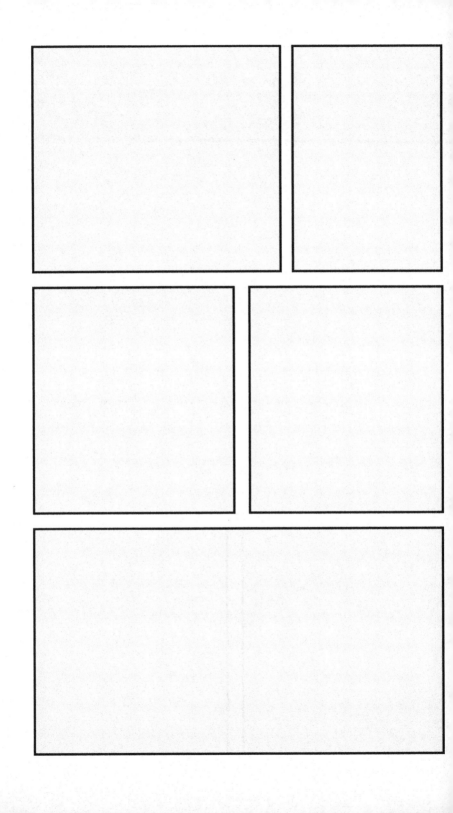

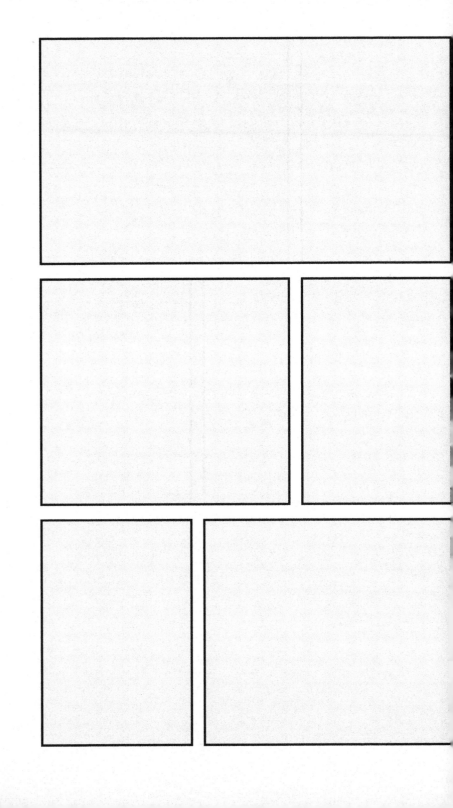

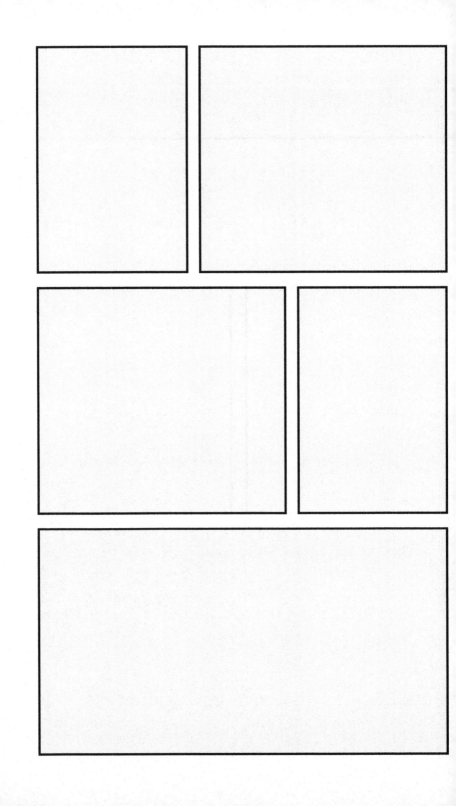

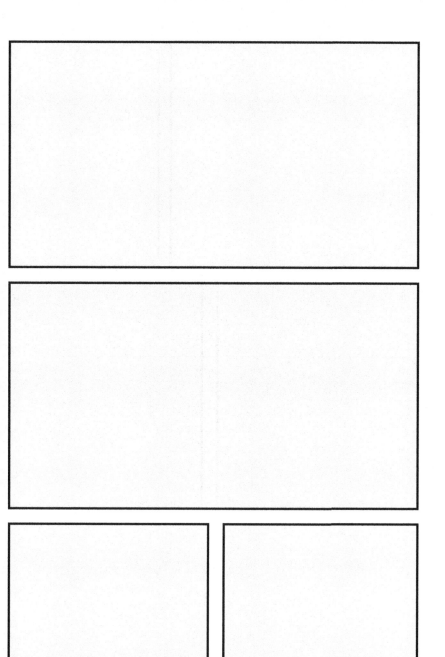

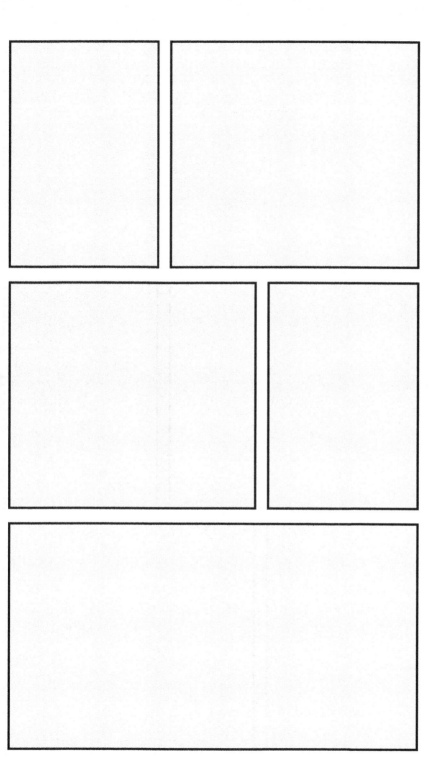

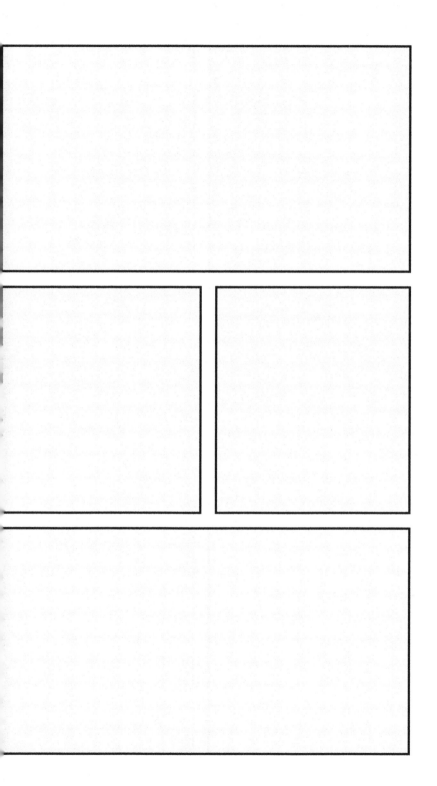

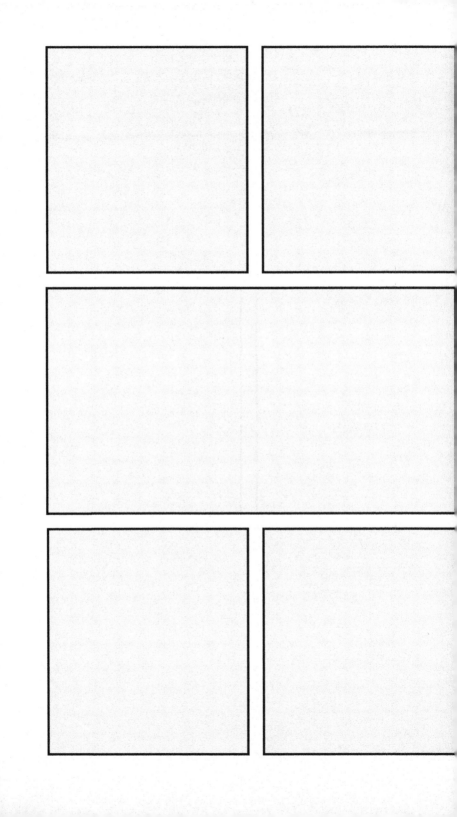

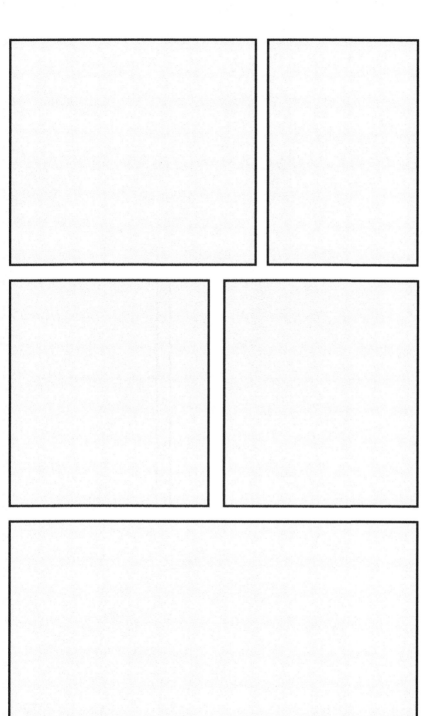

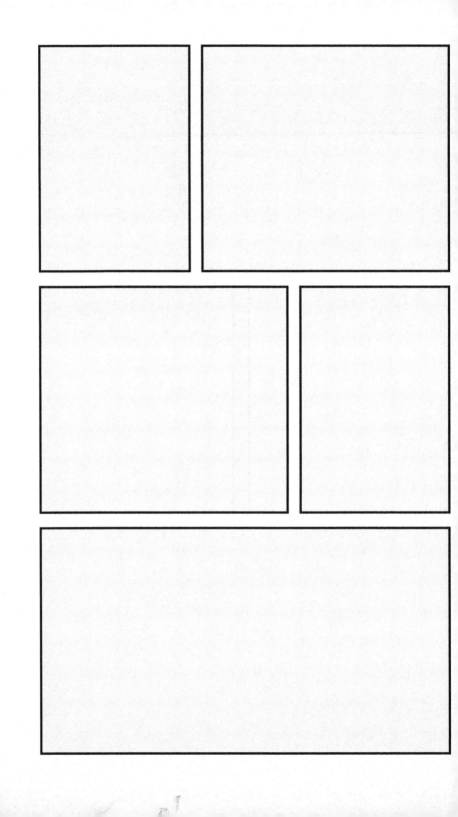

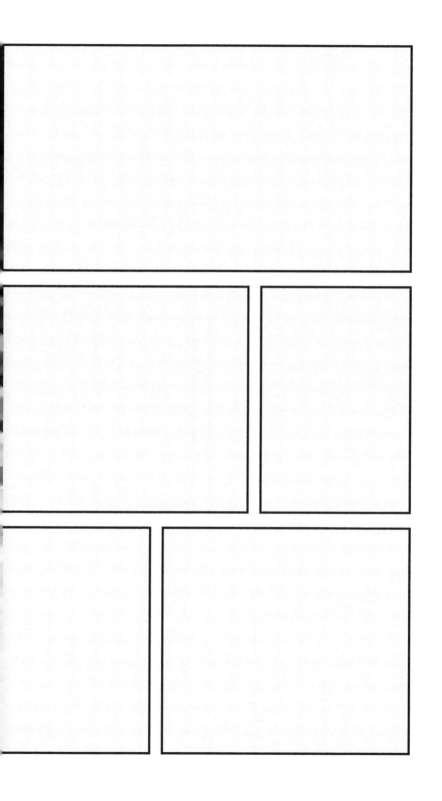

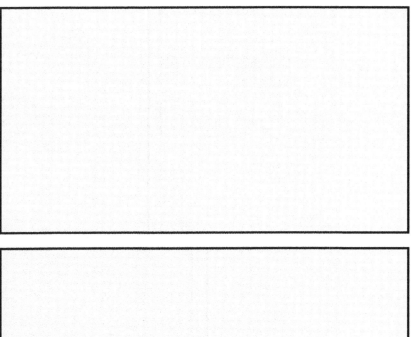

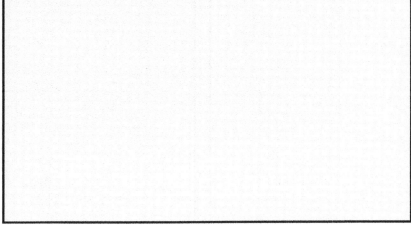

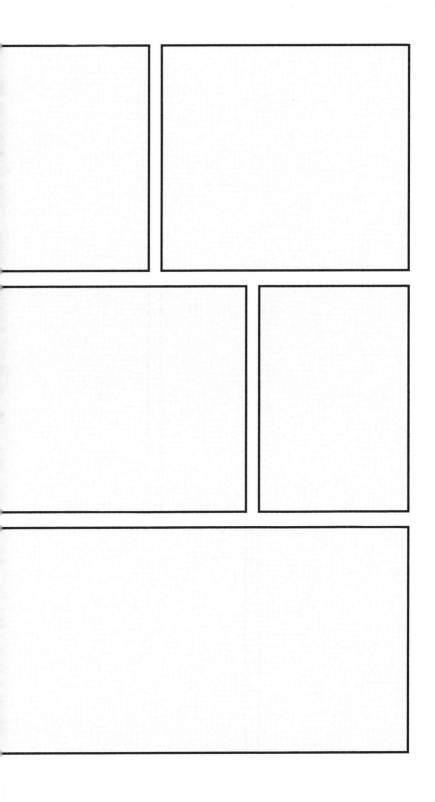

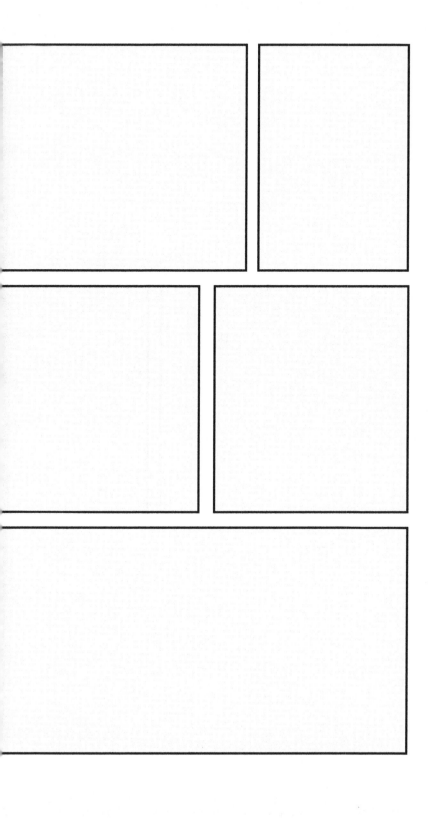

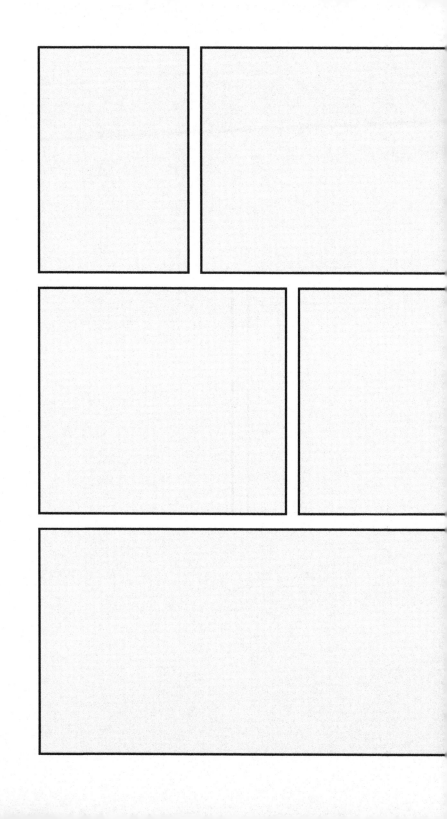

# Notes :

# Notes :

# Notes :

# Notes :

# Notes :

Made in United States
Orlando, FL
19 April 2023

32235977R00046